To Mel

from,  The

Traveler's Poet

Travels Through Nature and Life

May God bless you
And keep you in His care

.... "Enjoy

MICHAEL
BARNAUSKAS

Michael P. Barnauskas
The Traveler's Poet

Acknowledgements

I want to thank my family for the love and support given me, especially my sister Marie.

I want to thank the Veteran's Administration and the VA Medical Center in Wilkes-Barre, PA for treatment and care given me as well as treatment to all veterans of this great land.

I also want to thank the Scranton Counseling Center, the people who I have worked with over the years, and everyone who showed me love and kindness.

Most humbly, I want to thank God for delivering me from many dangers and pitfalls, giving me salvation and this rich, abundant live. Rich, not as the world counts richness, but rich in the kingdom of God. I also want to acknowledge that all good things come from God as He in His word tells us so.

The Traveler's Poet

Throughout life's journey
Are gathered from joy and sorrow
Trials and tribulation
These thoughts now put into words
May the reader of this collection of poems
Experience a rose that was born
Amidst a bed of thorns.

Notice to a Princess

Where is your glass slipper, Cinderella?
It is almost dawn
One less pumpkin in the pumpkin patch
My heart is also gone
Sped swift in cleft of wings
Arrival-departure, sudden and strange
The fate of rendezvous perhaps
Not braid of wedding rings
Fairy Godmothers pre-arrange
Time is not a cruel intriguer
Fond to mystify romance
But reminiscence builds minds of dreamers
This tangent world thus enhanced
Midnight sets not afire stars
Distant beacons of twinkling light
Yet the glimmer that transpires deepen darkness
Shall rise one's soul to Heaven's height
Pain and sorrow of this world
At times seem too hard to bear
But hope breaks through tomorrow
And lifts from the depths of despair
Strife's waters toss relentless churn
Requite of victory and defeat
Life's mysteries vie to be discerned
Midst tides of bitter beside the sweet
Dust-stained cheek and teardrop eyes
Are not reproof of one who fails

True worth so oft' disguised
Abides beneath indignant veils
Behold the union Rose and Thorn
Creation's visage to the wise
A reed despised, distained, held in scorn
Crowned and praised
God's glorious, beautiful reprise

Dearest Moon, The Stars

I have counted the stars of endless nights
And watched them beam twinkling light
Across the great expanse of space
While to ends of all creation they race
But who can count the days
Each star has shone
Or grasp the distance light was thrown
Not I, not I, I cannot reach the sky
I am captured by their splendor
But to touch them, no not I
Yet if I could show you how I see them
While on a leisure night
Just as in my childhood days
They are the same, they have not changed
Though I have traveled many miles
And wandered many ways
And if I could but proclaim the mystery
My desiring heart beholds
When I gaze into an evening sky
And see these specks of shining gold
I often wondered why God made them
Are they there for you and me
To just watch or perhaps to wish upon
Or are they landing zones for Angels
Like islands in the sea

Lonely is the Wind

Can't tell you where it's going
Only show you damage where it's been
If it's any help worth knowing
Lonely is the wind
Lonely is the wind that blows
Cross valleys, plains and mountain tops
Blowin', not knowin' where it goes
Ever bellowing but never making a friend
Yes lonely, lonely is the wind
Lonely the wind that streaks on by
Chasing clouds and birds cross a peaceful sky
Ever moanin' but not knowin' why
Lonely its only reply
Lonely is the wind that smashes rocks
Of cliffs and strides of mountain tops
Ever blowin' it keeps on goin'
And never stops
Lonely, lonely is the wind

Butterflies

Butterflies through the skies
Flying to and fro
With no hello or goodbyes
We know not where they go
But butterflies to our surprise
Come and go too soon
A pleasant sight for our eyes
They take away the gloom

A Kitten

Is about "that big" with paws
Each one consisting of claws
Has a head that is almost round
Pink nose where whiskers abound
Pointed ears and sparkling eyes
A birth certificate declaring 9 lives
Is part of the heart of a child
Warm, loving, playful and mild
And I guess you can call it friend
Fur on its back, tail on its end
It follows you wherever you go
But only if you run slow
'Cause kittens don't run very fast
And can easily get lost in the grass

Like Fur to a Kitten

May a river that runs forever
Carry you along the way
Of happiness and laughter
And bright sunshiny days
May blossoms of the springtime
Be yours to display
Angels up in heaven
Nigh to hear you pray
May there be the pleasant morning
You awaken to robin's song
Gentle be the warning
That keeps from doing wrong
May God bless and keep you
And help you be strong
And, like fur to a kitten
May you always belong

Fireflies

Did you ever watch fireflies
Across fields like stars beneath the skies
Did you ever try to catch them
I guess it's just their sheer surprise
All at once they blink and seem to wink
And it makes us lift our lazy eyes
When all things it seems depart
And sleep steps in to steal the heart
I guess for then God thought it wise
And thus inspired fireflies

That Pumpkin Jack O'Lantern

Orange because he was born that way
But happy because he's in style
And there's somethin' about him
That makes us all love him
The pumpkin with a smile
Children rescue him in autumn
From a place inside the fence
To save him from a pie crust
Cause some people have no sense
Always dressed for show time
He appears in his best
In the window with a candle
Where he welcomes every guest
And on hayrides and Halloweening
He's the words of our song
Symbol of the joy we share
The pumpkin who can do no wrong
So with respect and admiration
We acknowledge his acclaim
And place that pumpkin Jack O'Lantern
Into the fall of fame

The Sojourn of Summer ◆ Conquest of Autumn ◆ Farewell

Stood an army of fragrant flowers
Fields of clover in morning dew
Kissed by sunshine, blessed with showers
They sweetened the air a season through
Standing watch into the wind
Branches of trees so green
Waved to birds "come dwell within"
Sheltered boughs where they could sing
The charm of summer's magic spell
Cast upon the land its part
A breeze to penetrate each dell
And warm the traveler's restless heart
Over meadows verses rhymed
Unrehearsed, broadcast on wind
Recorded live by sea of time
Kept on file deep within
So in grief branches call
Birds depart in hasten flight
Soon in blood each leaf shall fall
By autumn's sword swift as night
When in defeat the rose is withered
Crushed by autumn's bold array
Leaves upon the ground lie scattered
Golden memories of yesterday
Farewell to her dreams and stories told
Summer's gone but we pause a while
For only hearts cruel and cold
Will not look back on her and smile

A Veterans' Day Parade

It's a Veterans' Day Parade
And in shade of Old Glory
Americans tell the story
In thoughts of peace
Memories of war
As our flag waves on before
Sense of dignity
Sense of pride
Marching along side by side
Though a cloudy day in November
All of us still remember
Our Veterans on Veterans' Day

Thanksgiving Day

Oh blow ye winds of November
Take leaves from the trees
Strip them bare
Take and freeze last remnants of summer
But remember be gentle and fair
Give time for forest creatures to gather
Last stash of nuts and stow away
Time for migrant birds to spread
Fluttering wings and fly away
And to gentle folk who know what matters
Give memories, God's blessings to share
When at the table all gather
To thank and praise our maker
On that special Thanksgiving Day

The First Snowfall

Tender snowflakes fall
To touch against your face
And rest upon your shoulders like a shawl
When summer gives its place
To old winter's call
A gray squirrel makes it to his hide-a-way
In some treetop tall
You raise your hands up to your nose and chin
Brushing away snow that gathers
Every now and then
Always thinking what all begins
With the first snowfall

Winter Sleep

Winter snow fallen down
Covers frozen ground
Trees no longer bare
Sport covering of winter hair
Spell cast all around
No trace of summer can be found
All is calm, not a sound
Winter sleep so profound

Paint

Amazing what to do with paint
Paint a picture of what is
Or what "aint"
Make a summer scene
Midnight sky, stars that gleam
Sky of blue, trees so green
Silver moon with moonbeam
Flowers of many colors
Tulips and hyacinths of spring
Winter hillside, snow of white
Autumn's sheer delight
Mountains tall, that's not all
Get a brush and on the wing
You can paint most anything

The Christmas Tree

In most every home at Christmas Time
Tradition commemorates the season
When we gather round to celebrate
Finding it oh so pleasing
As joyously we decorate
The cherished Christmas Tree
Dressed from top to bottom
Ornaments, string of lights
Shining tinsel, graceful garland
What a beautiful sight
And we can always remember
Moments warm and tender
Spent with loved ones near
At winter's time of year
Though cold and drear
Our delight will always be
Tradition of the Christmas Tree

Memories

Memories held dear
Remnants of yesteryears
Going back to the used-to-be
Filling eyes with loving tears
Memories left behind
Ever resonate on the mind
And friends once dear
Remain ever near
When I look back I am touched
In my heart they mean so much
With regards to the past
May those memories forever last

Near and Dear

Tonight, my soul in flight
I caught glimpse of
A distant star
When in the pines aloft a light
Shone down this world
Of ours
Clouds of rolling clouds
Tried hard to spoil the view
But the swollen tide
Brushed aside
When I thought of you

My Valentine

Till rivers cease to run
And children no longer play
Robins hush their song
Of treetop serenade
When roses no longer wait for
Tomorrow's kiss of morning dew
Posies no more offer
Thoughts warm, kind and true
Till ships come into harbor
No one to sail the ocean blue
A pledge of love is offered
In this valentine for you

One Little Rose

I tossed a rose onto the river
For today I am alone
I watched the waters receive it
The angel my silent prayer
God speed to my love and deliver it
Handle with care
As a seed it was implanted
In my heart long ago
Fulfillment to be granted
As on, the waters flow
Give to my love all my longing
This much I'm certain she'll know
That to my heart belonging there is
This one little rose

How to Touch a Rose

Tenderly with breath held
Does one stretch forth his hand
Carefully
Mindful of the thorns
And the promise deep
That all must keep
To be gentle and kind
How does one touch a rose
Softly, mildly petals rest
As a dove within the nest
Hands held nigh
Close to the breast
While breathing a sigh
Does one stretch forth and touch
This sacramental symbol of love

Precious

Precious is the ray of sunlight
Whose touch brings forth
A blossom to unfold
Precious is the flame of love light
When warmth enjoins
A treasure we behold
And precious are the little flowers
That adorn the earth on which we trod
Precious, precious are the little children
Who adorn the throne of God

What Makes a Home

More than siding covered walls
And chimney tall
More than curtain hung windows
To see through
More than a sight with beautiful view
More than kitchen table and chairs
More than basement, attic and upstairs
True as it's said there is more
It takes love and a family
To make a home

What Matters

I'd rather take a slow walk
Down a country mile
See more to meet the eye
Than all this world counts worthwhile
I'd rather wake to songbirds' singing
Than horns, screeching brakes
And telephones ringing
I'd rather see trees
Leaves ruffling in the breeze
Than iPhones, computers
And all of life's tease
And flowers along the way
Can really make my day
The message I say and tell
I like it more than all the stores
Display and try to sell

Beauty

Beauty abounds in many things
And in everything it has a place
As in the sun, moon and stars
It's known to shine more from one
Than another's face
But beauty resounds in passive depths
Far greater than meets the eye
And once one has known it
He never forgets
No matter what time or the tides
May pass him by

The Beacon

A flame burns in the window
In the dark of night
The brave glow of one little candle
A quiet welcoming sight
As the great light that shone through the darkness
When God said to the darkness
Let there be light
And warmth proceeds from the flame
Like from a fire in a hearth
The warmth is the giving of the candle
In a fiery flame
The flame first attracts by its light
Then by its warmth
Drawing one closer to its comfort
Comfort of the presence of love
The flame in the candle of one's heart

Hope is

Like the flame of a candle
Flickering in the wind
Story that will never end
Fire that will not go out
'Midst tears, pain and doubt
And as years pass on
Its burning will go on and on
Yearning that will never part
The flame held deep in one's heart

The Treasure Chest of the Heart

The greatest treasure one has
Is in his heart
Moving him to do great things
Accomplishing works that last
In his life and that of others
Building cities but not of stone
Building relationships
And mending that which is broken
Extending life to that which has ended
Giving breath to death
Building a future with hope
Filling vials with precious memories
Touched by finger tips of emotion
Like feeling brail, a light in the darkness
We all hold these treasures within
By believing in the heart
Giving from the heart
Living and loving from your heart

Pray and Believe

When darkness surrounds you like a storm
And you feel alone and worn
When the sky turns all gray
And you can't find the way
When your heart is weary
Filled with grief and dismay
Do with diligence and sincerity
Seek the Lord and pray
With believing the clouds will break away
Sun begin to shine
And brighten up the day
Miracles do happen
This message to you I leave
Don't give up on God's answer
Only pray and believe

God's Poetry

In this world of come and go
A thought of wonder amazes me
The purpose for which rivers flow
Rings of time within a tree
The crust of earth with many folds
Islands at mercy in the sea
How journeys wind from tracks of old
And paths of strangers chance to meet
What exacts the matter of life's mold
And plots the course of destiny
This I ponder and behold
Words of God's poetry

Life's Own Victory Eternal

On the cross where Jesus lay
Hands fixed there with nails
I ponder bars of contradiction
Upon which unity prevails
In the heart of his conviction
Who am I that he should have died for me
Before I was even born or tried
Yet if in my repeated sin
I were to make him do it again
He thought it not a loss to forgive
For death is mine not his exhaustion

Eternity Trials

Greater competition of life's game is found
In those who must compete against themselves
In drugs, alcohol and loneliness
While spectators watch from linen covered shelves
Who is to say they are lost
Or they are ruined
When tossed they upon life's stormy sea
We watch, feet held fast upon dry land
For the test of the strong
Is not on the bleachers arm in arm
Eating popcorn and drinking soda pop
But down there in the bloody area
Where soldiers by the hundreds drop
So let more thought be given
As to just who is the living
For what is life but faith, hope, and love?
That which never dies
'Midst temptations tall and failing tries

A Columbus Voyage

Oh sky so desolate
Beneath your stormy gray I sigh
Lost, lost is the past
Washed to the swift and violent rage
Broken, fading, fainting
Bleak the memory now reseeding
Taken captive by the mist
Slowly rising into the gray
Little hulk of wood and sail
Enhanced to cross the ocean blue
Smile upon your bow, laughter in your trail
In your heart a dream
The compass to see you through
But do only fools set out beyond
safe reach of a comforting shore
Mortal thoughts of men cry out
Turn around and sail no more
Have faith! You seaman have faith!
Though dreams trail the darkness till dawn
Upon the horizon a harbor breaks
Sail on! Sail on! Sail on!

I Take Time to Dream

Yes, I take time to dream
Skip across worldly rooftops
And set my heart upon the wing
Yes I take time to dream
To rise above harden stone
Gather thoughts of teardrop softness
Responding to my heart's request
Like sweet caress of mourning dew
Yes I do. I take time to dream
I set my loft on a cloud
Stretched in God's heavenly nest
That cradles earth in a shroud
And dream. Yes I dream
I see star-drift mountain tops
Watch valley river streams
Winding loops of ribbon blue
That cross and bind pastures green
Dream, yes I tend to dream
Of forests dark and maidens fair
Of castles tall and moonlite nights
Of chivalry and valiant knights
In gallantry of those who dare
Threat reality through misty air
To dream....Yes!
I take time to dream

The Rose and the Thorn

Back to when we're born
We think upon our life
We have memories both good and bad
Happy moments, some sad
Tidings of joy, times of sorrow
For all this we can borrow
A lesson from the rose and thorn
Thorns prick and cause hurt
But roses make all the worth
Touch and feel the rose
Behold beauty and fragrant smell
Of this fondness never depart
Hold it close to your heart
And let the thorns cause not regret
Of them choose to avoid and forget

Kindness

A kind word is like a bird's
Sweet song
It lifts you up
Like a buttercup
And carries you along
A gentle touch
Can mean so much
When things go wrong
It makes you want to stay
Where you feel you belong

Unsaid Words

As we look back on our life
Somewhere in the past we may find
A moment when we should have said
A word or something birth in our heart
But not brought forth to share with another
We hesitated and the moment was lost
Oh if we knew the cost
Instead we go on with words unsaid
Perhaps it was a word of kindness
A pleasurable feeling we had toward another
A treasured pearl of great worth
Oh the hurt but for that word unsaid
We let it go by as we part
An unsaid word from the heart
I speak to you now my friend
This unsaid word in the end
I care about you
And you are dear to my heart
My friend

Be a Poet

With pen in hand write a poem
And to the world make it known
From memories of the past
Make those happenings last
Choose nature its work of art
Family and friends
Warm and loving in the heart
Take pen in hand write a poem
Of experience life has shown
Trials you've been through
That give you point of view
Sorrows and distress
What besets and depresses you
Joys and the happiness
And all that blesses you
A poem you can write
For all the world to see
Truth to stand the test of time
And readers respectfully will agree

Show Mildly Inner Love Externally

In your journey as you meet
Strangers on live's busy street
Shine a light that they may know
Delight in that gentle glow
That shines forth from your face
From recesses of your heart
Kind measures to them impart
Treasure to take along the way
Help them face a dreary day
And brother and sister gone astray
Don't forget when you pray
That you not be put to test
Forgive not judge you'll be blessed
Yes as you walk each weary mile
Give generously a gentle smile
And leave to God all the rest
In His will he know what's best

Heart to Heart

What does my heart say
Dear LORD as I pray
Searching deep inside
For what to confide
Discerning deep yearning
Of what to tell you
I ponder sincere
Knowing you are near
Waiting patiently
Listening to me
LORD may I be right
In your sight
Please answer me

True Riches

Greater wealth abounds
In righteousness deep
A token to impart
Passed not from the hand to hand
But from the heart

—**The Traveler's Poet**
M. P. B.

91644058R00029

Made in the USA
Columbia, SC
24 March 2018